Pork

.. OR ..

THE DANGERS OF PORK-EATING EXPOSED

BY J. H. KELLOGG, M.D.

GOOD HEALTH PUBLISHING COMPANY
BATTLE CREEK, MICHIGAN
1897

Pork: Or the Dangers of Pork-eating Exposed

Annotated Edition with current facts and comments included in italics.

Published in ©2017 by Waymark Books.

Waymark Books

P. O. Box 7

Cedar Lake, MI 48812-0007

www.waymarkbooks.com

ISBN #978-1611046953

Table of Contents

Dangers of Pork-Eating 4

A Dead Hog Examined 8

A Live Hog Examined 9

What is Lard? 13

Disgusting Developments 16

Where Scrofula Comes From 19

Origin of the Tape Worm 21

The Terrible Trichina 25

Pork Unclean 28

Evil Effects of Pork-Eating 30

Apologies for Pork-Eating Examined 35

What Shall We Do with the Hog? 38

Cases of Trichina Poisoning 39

Appendix: Current Facts about Hog Farms 42

Dangers of Pork-Eating

Pork-raising has come to be one of the great industries of this country; and since the supply is wholly regulated by demand, it may be taken as a proper index of the prodigious quantities of swine's flesh which are daily required to satisfy the gustatory demands of the American people. No other kind of animal food is so largely used as pork in its various forms of preparation.

The Yankee makes his Sunday breakfast of pork and beans, while the same article is a prominent constituent of at least two meals each day during the remainder of the week. Pork and hominy is almost the sole element of the Texan farmer; while in the Western states pork and potatoes constitute the most substantial portion of the farmer's bill of fare. The accompanying dish may be hominy, beans, or potatoes, but the main reliance is pork in each case.

> *"Americans, long devoted to chicken and beef, are eating more pork now than they have in years....According to the market research firm Euromonitor, sales of pork are up 20 percent in the United States since 2011." (Washington Post, "Why Americans Are Eating More Pork Now than They Have in Decades", 2017)*
>
> *In 2013, the meat industry processed 112 million hogs, according to NAMI. From those*

animals, U.S. meat companies produced 23.2 billion pounds of pork. Though meat consumption in the U.S. has dropped off slightly in recent years, at 270.7 pounds per person a year, we still eat more meat per person here than in almost any other country on the planet. In 2012, the average American consumed 71.2 pounds of red meat (beef, veal, pork, and lamb) and 54.1 pounds of poultry (chicken and turkey), according to the U.S. Department of Agriculture. (NBCNews.com)

"The U.S. per capita consumption of pork amounted to 50.1 pounds in 2016." (Statistica.com)

In the case of no other animal is so large a portion of the dead carcass utilized as food. It seems to be considered that pork is such a delicacy that not a particle should be wasted. The tails roasted; the snout, ears, and feet are pickled and eaten as souse; the intestines and lungs are eaten as tripe or made into sausages; black pudding is made from the blood; the liver, spline, and kidneys are so prized; the pancreas and other glands are considered great delicacies; while even the skin is made into jelly. In fact, nothing is left of the beast, not even the bristles, which the shoemaker claims. Surely it must be quite an important matter, and one well deserving attention, if it can be shown that an animal which is thus literally devoured, and that in such immense quantities,

Pork: Or the Dangers of Pork-eating Exposed

is not only unfit for food, but one of the prime causes of many loathsome and painful maladies. Let us examine the hog a little, and see what can be determined respecting his real nature, and his office in the economy of nature, if he has any.

- *By the end of the meat processing process, nearly 100 percent of a hog is used.*

- *Edible parts of a slaughtered pig are broken down into foods such as bacon and pork chops.*

- *Renderers, who collect and cook down even the hair off the hogs, "sell everything but the squeal."*

- *Bones, skulls, fat, and skin that will go on to other uses is crushed, then sent to a supercooker (a giant barrel-shaped deep fat fryer set at 270 degrees).*

- *Non-edible parts of the hob, which are broken down into fats and proteins, turn up in dozens of products, including pharmaceuticals (insulin and the blood thinner heparin are produced from hog byproducts, as are the "cillins," including amoxicillin, ampicillin and penicillin.)*

("Everything but the Squeal: How the Hog Industry Cuts Food Waste," NPR.org, 2014)

A Dead Hog Examined

Do you imagine that the repulsiveness of this creature is only on the outside? that within everything is pure and wholesome? Vain delusion! Sickening, disgusting, as is the exterior, it is, in comparison with what it covers, a fair cloak, hiding a mass of disease and rottenness which grows more superlatively filthy as we penetrate deeper and deeper beneath the skin.

On factory farms:

- *Pigs are forced to live in their own feces and vomit and even amid the corpses of other pigs.*

- *Conditions are so filthy that at any given time, more than one-quarter of pigs suffer from mange.*

- *Extremely crowded conditions, poor ventilation, and filth cause such rampant disease that 70% of pigs have pneumonia by the time they reach the slaughterhouse. (peta.org)*

A Live Hog Examined

Look at that object in a filthy mudhole by the roadside. At first, you distinguish nothing but a pile of black, slimy mud. The dirty mass moves! You think of a reptile, a turtle, some uncouth monster, reveling in his Stygian filth. A grunt! The mystery is solved. The sound betrays a hog. You avert your face and hasten by, sickened with disgust. Stop, friend, admire your savory ham, your souse, your tripe, your toothsome sausage in its native element. A dainty beast, isn't he!

Gaze over into that sty, our pork-eating friend. Have you done so before? and would you prefer to be excused? Quite likely; but we will show you a dozen things you did not observe before. See the contented brute quietly reposing in the augmented filth of his own ordure! He seems to feel quite at home, doesn't he?

Look a little sharper, and scrutinize his skin. Is it smooth and healthy? Not exactly so. So obscured is it by tetter, and scurf, and mange, that you almost expect to see the rotten mass drop off as the grunting creature rubs it against any projecting corner which may furnish him a convenient scratching-place. As you glance around the pen, you observe that all such conveniences have been utilized until they are worn so smooth as to be almost inefficient.

Rouse the beast, and make him show his gait. See how he rolls along, a mountain of fat. If he were human, he would be advised to chew tobacco for his obesity, and

Pork: Or the Dangers of Pork-eating Exposed

would be expected to drop off any day of heart disease. And so he will do, unless the butcher forestalls nature by a few days.

Indeed, not long ago a stout neighbor of his was quietly taking his breakfast from his trough, grunting his infinite satisfaction, when, without a moment's warning or a single premonitory symtom, his heart ceased to beat, and he instantly expired without finishing his meal, much to the disappointment of his owner, who was anticipating the pleasure of quietly executing him a few hours later, and serving him up to his pork-loving patrons. Suppose his death had been delayed a few hours, or rather, suppose the butcher had got the start of nature a little, as he generally contrives to do!

But we have not yet finished the examination of our hog. If you can possibly prevail upon yourself to sacrifice your taste in the cause of science, pork-loving friend, just clamber over into the reeking sty, and take a nearer view of the animal that is destined to delight the palates of some of your friends, perhaps your own. Make him straighten out his four legs. Now observe closely.

Do you see the open sore or issue, a few inches above his foot on the inner side? Do you say it is a mere accidental abrasion? Find the same on the other leg; it is rather a wise and wonderful provision of nature. Grasp the leg high up and press downward. Now you see its utility, as a mass of corruption pours out. That opening is the outlet of a sewer. Yes, a scrofulous sewer; and hence the offensive, ichorose matter which discharges from it. Should you fill a syringe with mercury of some colored injecting fluid, and drive the contents into this same opening, you would be able to trace all through the body of the animal little pipes communicating with it.

What must be the condition of the body of an animal so foul as to require a regular system of drainage to convey away its teeming filth? Sometimes the outlet gets closed by the accumulation of external filth. Then the ichorose stream ceases to flow, and the animal quickly sickens and dies unless the owner cleanses the parts, and so opens anew the feculent fountain, and allows the festering poison to escape.

What dainty morsels those same feet and legs make! What a delicate flavor they have, as every epicure asserts! Do you suppose the corruption with which they are saturated has any influence upon their taste and healthfulness?

Perhaps you are thoroughly disgusted now, and would like to leave the scene. Pause a moment. Now let us look at the inside of this wonderfully delicious beast!

- *The wastes collected and decomposing in pits directly beneath the hog pens pose extremely toxic hazards for animals and humans alike. As noted by the American Lung Association, "Animals have died and workers have become seriously ill in confinement buildings when hydrogen sulfide rises from agitated pits underneath. Several workers have died when entering a pit during or soon after the emptying process to repair pumping equipment. Persons attempting to rescue these workers have also died...." (American Lung Association)*

- *Researchers have documented an increase in respiratory, neurobehavioral, and mental illnesses among people living near factory hog farms. In a major study, narby residents of a large pig farm were found to have "higher reporting of headaches, runny noses, sore throats, excessive coughing, diarrhea, and burning eyes." A separate study determined that pregnant women and children are especially susceptible to factory farm emissions. treatment plant. (farmsanctuary.org)*

What is Lard?

Just under the foul and putrid skin we find a mass of fat from two to six inches in thickness, covering a large portion of the body. Now what is this? Lard, says one; animal oil; an excellent thing for consumptives; a very necessary kind of food in cold weather. Lard, animal oil, very truly; and, we will add, a synonym for disease, scrofula, torpid liver. Where did all that fat come from? or how happened it to be so heaped up around that poor hog? Surely it is not natural; for fat is only deposited in large quantities for the purpose of keeping the body warm in winter.

This fat is much more than is necessary for such a purpose, and is much greater in amount than ever exists upon the animal in a state. It is evidently the result of disease. So gross have been the habits of the animal, so great has been the foulness of his body, that its excretory organs—its liver, lungs, kidneys, skin, and intestines—have been entirely unable to carry away the impurities which the animal has been all its life accumulating.

And even the extensive system of sewerage, with its constant stream, which we have already described, was insufficient to the task of purging so vile a body of the debris which abounded in every organ and saturated every tissue. Consequently this great flood of disease, which made the blood black, turbid current, was crowded out of the veins and arteries into the tissues, and there accumulated as fat! Delectable morsel, a slice of fat pork, isn't it? Concentrated, consolidated filth!

Then the fatter the hog, the more diseased he is?— Certainly. A few years ago, there were on exhibition at the great cattleshow in England a couple of hogs which had been stuffed with oil-cake until they were the greatest monsters of obesity ever exhibited. Of course they took the first premium; and if premium had been awarded to the animals which were capable of producing the most disease, it is quite probable that they would have headed the list still.

Lard, then, obtained from the flesh of the hog by heating, is nothing more than extract of a diseased carcass! Who that knows its character would dare to defile himself with this "broth of abominable things"?

According to onegreenplanet.org:

- *Using antibiotics and other drugs, pigs have been systematically bred and modified to be fat. In 2009, about 80 percent of the antibiotics sold in the United States went to livestock. The average pig within a factory farm weighs 215.5 pounds.*

- *Breeding sows, which are restrained in unbedded 18-24 inch-wide crates where they are unable to walk or even turn around during their entire pregnancies,*

What is Lard?

average 600-900 pounds. The sow is fed at one ened of the crate, while feces collects at the other. Deprived of all exercise and any opportunity to fulfill her behavioral needs, such sows live in a constant state of distress. (Humane Farming Association)

Disgusting Developments

Now let take a little deeper look, prepared to find disease and corruption more abundant the deeper we go. Observe the glands which lie about the neck. Instead of being their ordinary size, and composed of ordinary gland structure, we find them surrounded by large masses of scrofulous tissue. Perhaps tuberculous degeneration has already taken place. If so, the soft, cheesy, infectious mass is ready to sow broadcast the seeds of consumption and premature death. For, according to some excellent authorities, tuberculous disease is capable of communication by means of tubercles. If the animal is of sufficient age, the further process of ulceration will have occurred.

Now take a deeper look still, and examine the lungs of this much-prized animal. If he is more than a few months old, you will be likely to find large numbers of tubercles. If he is much more than a year old, you will be more likely than not to find a portion of the lung completely consolidated. Yet all of this filthy, diseased mass is cooked as a delicious morsel, and served up to satisfy fastidious tastes. If the animal had escaped the butcher's knife a few years, he would have died of tuberculous consumption.

But what kind of a liver would you expect such an animal to have? Is not excessive fatness one of the surest evidences of a diseased and inactive liver?—Infallible. Then a fat hog must have a dreadfully diseased bile manufactory.

Disgusting Developments

Make a cut into its substance. In seventy-five cases out of a hundred you will find it filled with abscesses. In a large percentage still will be found the same diseased products which seem to infect every organ, every tissue, every structure of the animal. Yet these same rotten, diseased, scrofulous livers are eaten and relished by thousands of people who cannot express their contempt for the Frenchman who eats a horse or a Chinaman who dines upon fricasseed puppy.

Now just glance at the remaining contents of the abdomen. In every part you notice evidences, unmistakable, of scrofula, fatty degeneration, and tuberculous masses.

- *Extremely crowded conditions, poor ventilation, and filth cause such rampant disease that 80% of pigs contract pneumonia by the time they reach the slaughterhouse.*

- *"Nearly 70% of swine confinement workers experience one or more symptoms of respiratory illness or irritation... The turnover rate of swine confinement workers is very high, and some owners have had to sell their operations because they could not work in their own units..." (American Lung Association, in collaboration with the University of Iowa)*

- *Italian researchers who investigated the health of 10,041 slaughtered pigs from 91 different farms found that 59.6% of the animals had lung lesions. They also determined that the presence of lung lesions was directly correlated with lower carcass quality. (Journal of Veterinary Medicine, March 2007)*

Where Scrofula Comes From

The word scrofula is derived from the Latin *scrofa*, which means a sow. The ancient Romans evidently believed that scrofula originated with the hog, and hence they attached the name of the beast to the disease. Saying that a man has scrofula, then, is equivalent to saying that he has the hog disease. After we have seen that the hog is the very embodiment of scrofulous disease, can any one doubt the accuracy of the conclusion of the Romans who named the disease?

Notes from the Iowa State University, College of Veterinary Medicine website regarding tuberculosis in swine:

- *Scrofula, a disease involving glandular swelling, it thought to be a form of tuberculosis.*

- *In the United States, tuberculosis once was a common disease in swine.*

- *A major effort to eradicate tuberculosis in cattle and in people markedly reduced the incidence of the types of tuberculosis in swine as well.*

- *Increasing prevalence of tuberculosis in immunocompromised people, together with resistance of tuberculosis to many*

> *antibiotics, has brought this disease back into the public eye.*
>
> - *In recent years, avian (bird-related) tuberculosis has been found in not only confinement-raised swine, but people.*
> - *This reappearance of tuberculosis in hogs has caused significant condemnation losses to pork producers.*
>
> Iowa State University
School of Veterinary Medicine website

Origin of the Tape Worm

We shall attempt to trace the history of this horrid parasite only so far as concerns its introduction into the human system.

With this end in view, let us glance again at the diseased liver. It will be no uncommon thing if we discover numberless little sacs, or cysts, about the size of a hemp seed. These do not present a very formidable appearance, certainly; but as soon as they are taken into the human stomach, the gastric juice dissolves off the membranous sac, and liberates a minute animal, which had been lurking there for months, perhaps, awaiting this very opportunity.

This creature, although very small, is furnished with a head and four suckers, and as it passes on into the intestines, the little suckers attach themselves firmly to the wall of the intestines, and the parasite begins to grow. In a short time an addition to its body is produced posteriorly, attached like a joint. Soon a duplicate of this appears, and then another, and another, until the body attains a length of several yards. Not infrequently tapeworms measuring thirty to one hundred feet in length are found in the intestines of human beings.

Under some circumstances the eggs of the tapeworm find entrance into the body, when the disease is developed in another form. The embryonic worms consist of a pair of hooklets so shaped that a twisting motion will cause them to penetrate the tissue after the fashion of a corkscrew. Countless numbers of these may be taken into the system, since a single tapeworm has been found to produce more than two million eggs.

By the boring motion referred to, which seems to be spontaneous in the young worm, the parasites penetrate into every part of the body. Penetrating the walls of the blood-vessels, they are swept along in the life-current, thus finding their way even to the most delicate structures of the human system. They have been found in all the organs of the body, even the brain and the delicate organs of vision not escaping the depredations of this destructive parasite.

When this lively migrating germ gets fully settled in the tissues, it becomes enveloped in a little cell, and remains quiet until taken into the stomach of some other animal, when it is liberated, and speedily develops into a full-grown tapeworm, as already described. But although quiet, the imprisoned parasite is by no means harmless.

The cysts formed often attain such a size as to endanger life. When developed in the eye, they occasion blindness; in the lungs or other organs, they interfere with the proper functions of the organs, in the liver, which is the most frequent rendezvous of these destructive creatures, a most serious and fatal disease known as hydatids is occasioned by the extraordinary development of the cysts, which are originally not larger than a pea, but by excessive growth assume enormous proportions. The same disease may occur in any other part of the body in which the germs undergo development.

Origin of the Tape Worm

The germs of these dreadful animals are found not only in the liver, but in other organs as well. Pork containing them is said to be "measly." Sometimes the condition is discovered; but that such is not always the case is evidenced by the fact that the tapeworm is every year becoming more frequent. It has long been common in Germany. In Iceland it has become extremely common. In Abyssinia the occurrence of the worm has become so frequent, owing to the bad dietetic habits of the people, that it has been said that every Abyssinian has a tapeworm. In this country the parasite is most common among butchers and cooks.

Some time since, we received from a friend in the South a specimen of pork which was so densely peopled with the germs of this dreadful parasite that every cubic inch of flesh contained more than a score of them. The writer has in his microscopical cabinet specimens of the embryonic worms taken from hydatid tumors of the liver of a patient who died of the disease in Bellevue Hospital, New York.

The poor victim who is forced to entertain this unwelcome guest suffers untold agonies, and finally dies, if he cannot succeed in dislodging the parasite.

Notes from the Alberta, Canada, Department of Agriculture and Forestry website:

- *Despite the fact that incidences of tapeworm are now rare in Canadian and American swine herds, more than 1,000*

> *human cases are still reported annually in the United States.*

- *Many of these human cases result after travel outside Canada and the United States.*
- *The cycle begins with swine eating food or drinking water contaminated with eggs from human feces.*
- *The tapeworm attaches to the human intestine by its "head," called a scolex. The tapeworm grows to a length of 2-7 meters within 5-12 weeks.*
- *The pork tapeworm can live for over 20 years, generating several thousand eggs daily.*
- *One tapeworm can shed up to 300,000 eggs per day.*

The Terrible Trichina

Now, my friend, assist your eyesight by a good microscope, and you will be convinced that you have only just caught a glimpse of the enormous filthiness, the inherent badness, and intrinsic ugliness of this loathsome animal. Take a thin slice of lean flesh; place it upon the stage of your microscope, adjust the eyepiece, and look. You will see displayed before your eyes hundreds of voracious little animals, each coiled up in its little cell, waiting for an opportunity to escape from its prison walls and begin its destined work of devastation.

An eminent gentlemen in Louisville has made very extensive researches upon the subject, and asserts that in at least one hog out of every ten these creatures may be found. A committee appointed by the Chicago Academy of Medicine to investigate this subject reported that they found in their examination at the various packing-houses in the city one hog in fifty infested with trichina. Other investigations have shown a still greater frequency of the disease.

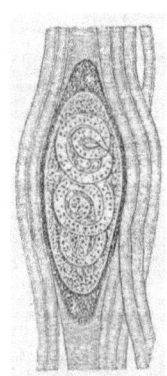

A few years ago I obtained a small portion of the flesh of a person who had died from trichina poisoning.

Upon subjecting it to a careful microscopical examination with a good instrument, I discovered multitudes of little worms. Each individual presented the appearance shown in the accompanying accurate engraving.

The animal is there seen enclosed in a little cyst, or sac, which is dissolved by the gastric juice when taken into the stomach. The parasite, being thus set at liberty, immediately penetrates the thin walls of the stomach, and gradually works its way through the whole muscular system. It possess the power of propagating its species with wonderful rapidity, and a person once infected is almost certain to die a lingering death of excruciating agony.

In Helmstadt, Prussia, one hundred and three persons were poisoned in this way, and twenty of them died within a month.

It is doubtless not known how many deaths are really due to this cause; for many persons die of strange, unknown diseases, which baffle the doctors' skill both as to cure and diagnosis. Trichinosis very much resembles various other diseases in some of its stages, and is likely to be attributed to other than its cause. It is thought by prominent medical men that hundreds of people die of the disease without suspecting its true nature.

Trichinosis facts from Medicine.net

- *Eating raw or undercooked pork infected with the larvae of a parasitic worm is one cause of trichinosis.*

- *Initial symptoms of trichinosis may include abdominal discomfort, nausea, diarrhea, vomiting, fatigue, and fever.*

The Terrible Trichina

- *The severity of symptoms depends on the number of infectious worms consumed in the meat.*
- *Although 90-95% of trichinosis infections result in either minor symptoms or no complications, the following serious symptoms may result:*
    - *Heart muscle inflammation (myocarditis)*
    - *Pulmonary problems such as cough, shortness of breath, or lung hemorrhage (lung bleeding).*
    - *A diverse range of central nervous system problems, which may include confusion, delirium, ataxia, seizures, vertigo, auditory and speech changes along with many other neurological deficits.*
- *For some patients, these complications can slowly resolve over six months, while in others, they may persist for years.*

Pork Unclean

Have we not seen that the hog is nothing better than an animated mass of physical defilement? Few who have seen the animal will dispute that his filthiness is a most patent fact. How wise and sanitary, then, was the command of God to the ancient Jews: "It is unclean unto you. Ye shall not eat of their flesh nor touch their dead carcasses."

Although it may not be said that this law still exists, and is binding as a moral obligation, it is quite plain that the physical basis upon which the law is founded is as good today as at any previous period. Could it be proved that the hog had kept pace with advancing civilization, and had improved his habits, we might possibly feel more tolerance for him; but he is evidently just as unclean as ever, and just as unfit for food.

Adam Clarke, when once requested to give thanks at a repast of which pork constituted a conspicuous part, used the following words: "Lord, bless this bread, bless these vegetables, and this fruit; and if thou canst bless under the gospel what thou didst curse under the law, bless this swine's flesh."

The Mohammedans, as well as the Jews, abstain entirely form the use of pork. Such is also the case with some of the other tribes of Asia and Africa.

A 2007 survey by the Pew Research Center found that:

- *Nine-in-ten U.S. Muslims say they never eat pork*
- *Most U.S. Jews (57%) say they do eat pork.*

As a point of faith, members of the Seventh-day Adventist Church do not eat pork.

Evil Effects of Pork-Eating

At the head of the list we place *scrofula*. How almost universally it abounds. How do chronic sore eyes, glandular enlargements, obstinate ulcers, disfigured countenances, unsightly eruptions, including the long list of skin diseases, all proclaim the defilement of the blood with this vile humor. So, too, do the vast army of dwarfed, strumous, precocious children tell the same story.

Erysipelas: Erysipelas, too, a dreadful scourge, owes more to pork than to any other predisposing cause.

> *Erysipelas is an infectious disease mostly of growing or adult swine. It may be clinically inapparent, may cause acute illness involving many animals, or be a chronic disease characterized by enlarged joints, lameness, and endocarditis. (Iowa State University, College of Veterinary Medicine website)*

Leprosy: Leprosy, that terrible disease, so common in Eastern countries, and now beginning to show itself upon our own shores, is thought by many to be largely attributable to pork-eating.

> *Leprosy, a chronic infectious disease affecting especially the skin and peripheral nerves, is characterized by the formation of nodules that*

enlarge and spread accompanied by loss of sensation with eventual paralysis, wasting of muscle, and deformities.

In ancient times, the Egyptians believed that to drink pig's milk was believed to cause leprosy to the drinker. (Sacred-Texts.com)

Ellen G. White, one of the most prolific female writers of all time, wrote in the 1800's that: "God did not prohibit the Hebrews from eating swine's flesh merely to show his authority, but because it was not a proper article of food for man. It would fill the system with scrofula, and especially in that warm climate produce leprosy and disease of various kinds." (Selected Messages p. 417)

Biliousness: "Biliousness," a name which covers nearly every bad condition for which no appropriate name can be found, is notoriously the result of pork-eating. This is the main reason why so many people complain of biliousness in the spring, after gorging themselves with fat pork all winter. The liver is overworked in attempting to remove from the system such a mass of impurity as is received in eating pork. It consequently becomes clogged, congested, torpid. Then follow all the ills consequent upon the irritating effects of the accumulation of biliary matters in the blood. The skin becomes tawny and jaundiced. The kidneys are overworked. Perhaps fever results. A partial clearing out then occurs, which enables the individual to pass along for a time again until some epidemic of contagious disease claims him as its lawful victim.

> *Biliousness was a term used in the 18th and 19th centuries to describe bad digestion, stomach pains, constipation, and excessive flatulence (passing gas).*

> *Pork contains methionine, a sulfur-containing amino acid that produces "essence of rotting egg" as a fart byproduct. The Mayo Clinic adds that fat slows digestion, giving food more time to do its dirty work in your gut.*

Consumption: Consumption, is another disease which is not easily separable from pork-eating. In fact, scrofula is its great predisposing cause. The narrow chest, projecting shoulders, thin features, and lank limbs of so many young boys and girls are evidence of a consumptive tendency, of which a scrofulous diathesis is the predisposing cause.

> *Defined as an old and once common term for wasting away of the body, particularly from pulmonary tuberculosis.*

Dyspepsia: Dyspepsia, that malady of many forms, frequently results from the use of pork, especially when fat and salted or smoked pork, one of the most indigestible foods, is used. Pork requires between five and six hours for its digestion, while wholesome food will digest in half that time. This is the reason for the notion that salt pork is an excellent thing to "stick by the rib."

Defined as a malady whose symptoms when they are not typical of a well-described disease (for example, gastrointestinal reflux) and the cause is not clear.

Tapeworm: Tapeworm we have already mentioned as the result of eating measly pork. It is a very difficult disease to cure, and often baffles the best medical skill for many years. Few ever detect the cyst in the flesh of the hog unless their attention has been directed to the matter.

A parasite that enters the human digestive system and grows and thrives off what the human host consumes, causing severe weight loss or other digestive problems.

Trichinae: Trichinae produce in man an incurable disease. No remedy can stay the ravages of the parasite. All pork-eaters are in constant danger; for the worm is too small to be seen without the aid of the microscope. However, this disease is not so common, neither does it entail any weight of suffering upon posterity.

Pork: Or the Dangers of Pork-eating Exposed

Related to trichinosis, a disease caused by eating undercooked meat, usually pork, that contains trichinae, which develop as adults in the intestines and as larvae in the muscles, causing intestinal disorders, fever, nausea, muscular pain, and edema of the face.

Apologies for Pork-Eating Examined

On every hand we are met by all sorts of excuses for continuing to make swine's flesh an article of diet in spite of the striking evidences of its dangerous character, Let us examine a few of the most common of these apologies, and test their value.

Pork Is Necessary as a Heat-forming Food in Winter.—Are there not plenty of more healthful animals than hogs to supply all the animal fat necessary? Certainly there are; and, better still, we have the various grains and farinaceous vegetables, which are abundantly sufficient to furnish all the heat required by man in any latitude.

Our Fathers and Grandfathers Ate Pork, and yet Lived to very Old Age.—Ah? yes, my good friend, and you are suffering the penalty of their transgressions. You may not be aware of it yet; but more than likely your old age will not be so free from ills as was theirs. And quite as probably you may even now see in your children the results of your own, as well as your fathers' disregard of the dictates of sound sense in feasting upon the hog. Their frequent sore eyes, sore mouths, tetter, crysipelas, and other eruptions, are evidences of the scrofula which they have inherited.

Neither can you urge the plea, "Pork does not hurt me." No man ever became a drunkard who did not make the same excuse for liquor. You may not feel it now; but the future will expose your delusion.

The Hog is Clean if You Give Him a Chance to Be so.—It is surprising to us that anyone who knows anything of the real nature of a hog can make such an assertion. Who has not seen hogs wallowing in the foulest mire right in the middle of a green, fragrant clover pasture? The dirty creature will turn away from the nicest bed of straw to revel in a stagnant, seething mudhole. If one of his companions dies in the lot or pen, he will wait until putrefaction occurs, and then greedily devour the stinking carcass. The filthy brute will even devour his own excrement, and that when not unusually pressed by hunger.

The hog is by nature a scavenger, and is especially adapted for that purpose. Let him pursue his natural calling.

Sufficient Heat Will Kill the Trichinae and Incipient Tapeworms.—Surely, dead worms cannot kill any one; but it must be delightful for the pork-eater to contemplate his ham or sausage with the reflection that he is partaking of a diet of worms. The Frenchman sometimes eats earthworms; the African relishes lizards; and one philosopher so far overcame his natural prejudices as to eat spiders.

"How disgusting!" you say, and yet you shut your eyes and swallow a million monsters at a meal, because they are cooked, and so cannot bite. The louse-eating Patagonian cannot equal that. But it should be remembered that in order that the parasite should be killed, every part of the meat must be subjected to a heat of at least 2120 F., which is quite difficult to do, and is seldom accomplished. A whole family were poisoned by eating pork-chops which were well cooked upon the outside.

What Shall We Do with the Hog?

Stop raising him. Turn him loose. He will soon find his place, like the five thousand which ran down into the sea in the days of Christ.

If he must be raised, use him for illuminating our halls and homes. Lubricate our car and wagon axles with his abundant fat. Do anything with him but eat him. It would be dangerous to adopt the principle that we must devour everything which is in the way, or which cannot be otherwise utilized. Adam Clarke thought of one appropriate use to make of the hog. He said that if he were going to make an offering to the devil, he would employ a hog stuffed with tobacco.

Reader, what will you do? Can you continue to use as food such an abominable article as pork, and in so doing run so many risks as you must do? And if you decide that the animal is unfit to claim a place upon your own table, can you conscientiously raise and sell him, to your neighbors' injury?

Cases of Trichina Poisoning

The reported cases of death from this terrible cause have become so frequent that we are no longer startled by them. Ten years ago the description of the death of a person literally infested with worms, and tortured to death by their inroads upon the system, would have excited feelings of deepest horror; but these accounts have now become so common that little interest is shown in them, and death from this cause is one of the regular causes of additions to the mortuary list. Nevertheless, the disease is divested of none of its real horrors by its common occurrence.

No one is safe; anyone who uses swine's flesh as food in any form is liable to the disease. Salting, smoking, and the other ordinary means of curing pork do not destroy the parasite.

A few years ago, Dr. Germer, health officer of Erie, Pa., was sent for in haste to see a patient who was supposed to be suffering from cholera. He hastened to the bedside, and found a whole family sick with symptoms much resembling those of cholera, though the season was then midwinter.

Suspecting the possible cause, he secured a specimen from the pork barrel, and hastened to his office. Upon making a careful microscopic examination, he found myriads of the loathsome parasites in every part of the flesh examined. The writer prepared numerous microscopic specimens of the worm in various aspects

Pork: Or the Dangers of Pork-eating Exposed

from a portion of the infected meat kindly furnished by the doctor. These have been shown to hundreds of persons who were skeptical respecting the existence of such a pest.

In this case the hog had been fattened on the premises, having been purchases when quite young by the owner, a German, from a drove of hogs which passed through the city. It was known that, previous to the purchase of the hog, two of the drove had died on the road, and had been devoured by their scavenger companions. No doubt the deaths were the result of the trichinosis; and by devouring the victims the whole herd became infected.

It would be difficult to estimate what an amount of suffering and death was entailed by the consumption of this great herd of trichinous hogs. Several members of the German family died, together with several of the neighbors. Those who survived the acute stages of the disease escaped only to linger out a painful existence in the chronic and incurable state of the malady.

Some three years later the writer received a specimen of pork from a gentleman in Wisconsin who requested an examination of the same, stating that he procured it from the pork barrel of a neighbor whose family were suffering from a disease which the doctors called cholera infantum.

Several of the children had died, and other members of the family were still dangerously ill. The pork had been suspected and examined, but no trichinae were found by the observers, though several physicians had inspected it. Upon making a careful microscopical inspection of the specimen, it was found to be alive with young trichinae.

THE END.

Appendix: Current Facts about Hog Farms

- *Pigs are forced to live in their own feces and vomit and even amid the corpses of other pigs. Conditions are so filthy that at any given time, more than one-quarter of pigs suffer from mange.*

- *Piglets, who are taken away from their distraught mothers after just a few weeks, have their tails chopped off, their teeth are clipped off with pliers, and the males are castrated—all without painkillers.*

- *In 1995, 25 million gallons of hog urine and feces spilled into a North Carolina river, immediately killing more than 10 million fish. To get around water pollution limits, factory farms frequently convert tons of urine and feces into liquid waste, which they then spray into the air. This manure-filled mist is carried away by the wind and inhaled by the people who live nearby.*

- *In order to promote unnaturally fast growth and prevent death from disease, pigs are fed a steady diet of the same antibiotics that are depended on to treat human illnesses, a practice which has led to the development of "superbacteria," or antibiotic-resistant bacterial strains.*

Appendix: Current Facts about Hog Farms

- *A typical slaughterhouse kills up to 1,100 pigs every hour, which makes it impossible for them to be given humane, painless deaths. The U.S. Department of Agriculture documented 14 humane slaughter violations at one processing plant, where inspectors found hogs who "were walking and squealing after being stunned [with a stun gun] as many as four times." Because of improper stunning methods and extremely fast line speeds, many pigs are still alive when they are dumped into scalding-hot hair-removal tanks—they literally drown in scalding-hot water.*

- *The images are graphically clear: Small piglets being hurled to a concrete floor; large, fully grown sows gnawing the bars on their tiny cages; pigs with open sores lying untended on the ground; piglets squealing as their tails are cut off without benefit of anesthetic; and workers tossing live piglets back and forth and describing them as "bouncy." (ABC News, "Iowa Pig Farm Filmed, Accused of Animal Abuse, 2011)*

Pork: Or the Dangers of Pork-eating Exposed

www.ingramcontent.com/pod-product-compliance
Lightning Source LLC
Chambersburg PA
CBHW050047080526
44586CB00014B/1492